THE WEAVE ROOM

for Courtney,

Good to meet you

at Elon.

Mike

10/30/98

PHOENIX **POETS**

A SERIES EDITED BY ALAN SHAPIRO

Michael Chitwood (signature)

MICHAEL CHITWOOD

the weave room

THE UNIVERSITY OF CHICAGO PRESS

Chicago and London

Michael Chitwood is a freelance journalist whose work appears regularly in a number of newspapers as well as on North Carolina's largest National Public Radio affiliate. He is the author of two books of poetry: *Salt Works* (1992) and *Whet* (1995).

The University of Chicago Press, Chicago 60637
The University of Chicago Press, Ltd., London
© 1998 by The University of Chicago
All rights reserved. Published 1998
Printed in the United States of America

07 06 05 04 03 02 01 00 99 98   1 2 3 4 5

ISBN 0–226–10397–8 (cloth)
      0–226–10398–6 (paper)

Library of Congress Cataloging-in-Publication Data

Chitwood, Michael.
      The weave room / Michael Chitwood.
            p. cm. — (Phoenix poets)
      ISBN 0-226-10397-8 (alk. paper). — ISBN 0-226-10398-6 (pbk.: alk. paper)
      I. Title. II. Series.
      PS3553.H535W43 1997   97-8422
      811′.54—dc21   CIP

for
the pattern-makers
Elaine Hall Chitwood and T. W. Chitwood, Jr.
and
the employees of the Angle Plant,
Rocky Mount, Virginia

Contents

THREE   *Threads*

Acknowledgments

Grateful acknowledgment is made to the editors of publications in which these poems, or versions of them, first appeared:

Brightleaf: "The Preaching"
DoubleTake: "The Day Ending and Beginning in the Afternoon," "A Fixer Quits," "Threads, End of Another Day," "The Thunderbolts of Zeus," "The Weaving"
North Carolina Literary Review: "In the Break Room," "The Men," "The Women," "Weave Room: What They Say"
Tar River Poetry: "Union"
Threepenny Review: "Lifting," "The Singing," "On the Roof of the Angle Plant"

The author wishes to thank three people who aided greatly in the writing of this book. Michael McFee read individual poems and, with his keen eye, helped to sharpen them. Alan Shapiro's fine and thorough critique of the early manuscript was essential to realizing the whole. And, Jean Chitwood provided the time to write, the greatest gift of all. To all three, much thanks.

ONE
Ties

The Silk Mill

was where he went everyday,
though, I didn't know, years past
using silk, but the old name
was as common in our house
as my own.
I didn't think of it as a building
as I didn't think of myself
as different from my name.
I was I and none other,
and The Silk Mill, capital T,
was like Heaven, capital H,
big, airy, filled with strings
that glittered and hummed.
The Silk Mill. It was
its syllables I first believed.

Ties

Uncles worked pocket knives
to rake the grease of work
from beneath their nails,
but yours, in the Sunday mirror
and quick at my throat,
were always clean.

Over, under, down through.
"The print or stripe should match the blue."

Sundays only
Granddad wore one.
Saturdays only
you did not.

Over, under, down through.
"You can judge a man by the shine on his shoes."

Granddad's hung
on the back of the bedroom door,
knotted all week.
Before services,
he'd cinch it and grin,
proud his boy felt this pinch
every working day.

My back against your chest,
you talked me into the knot,
over, under, down through.
Then you'd snug it
just short of choking
and call me "Mr. Chitwood,"
the name you dressed in
every morning to leave the house.

American Manhood versus American Bandstand

"Isn't she pretty?" he'd say to the TV
when the American Bandstand camera
zoomed in on Herman or one of the Hermits.
He'd just be passing through the living room
on the way back to the lawn or garden or car
or whatever he was doing,
which was always something
as it was always nothing for me,
privileged as I was to waste a morning
with the "unintelligible screeching of sissies."

My scalp bristled
from haircuts every other Friday night,
but underneath I was all Hermit,
or Raider or Rolling Stone
and he knew it,
which was why, I guess, he brought the story home,

that Hamilton boy, who'd had all the trouble and they said sold pot—did I
know anything about that?—anyway had hair to his shoulders and had been
told he'd have to wear a net, like the *other* women and don't you know he did
but must have taken it off, you know how lax third shift is, anything we say
at this table stays in the house, because last night he was working on a
loom in No. 2 when somebody hit the lever and that loom snatched a hank
clean from his scalp, slammed his head on the whip roller and took twelve
stitches to sew him up let that be a lesson to you.

But a lesson in what, I didn't know.
The dangers of working for him?
The proper use of hairnets?
The limits of stories as examples?
He didn't say
and I sang softly, "Yeah, yeah, yeah."

Singing the "Union Song" for the Company Man

It didn't matter that I'd seen
him waltz Mother around the kitchen,
singing "Hey, hey, good-looking, whatcha
got cooking," her batting at him
with the lid of the bean pot,
laughing, saying stop, meaning
don't. The pens flew
from his pocket shield on the dip.

It didn't matter that he put me
on his back and carried both poles,
the stringer, the light and me
up the dark river bank.
My hands clasped at his throat
could feel "Amazing Grace"
as he hummed it.

It didn't matter that he said "Stop"
and meant it. I'd get him going,
devil him, with that song,
"Look for the Union label,"
trying out the Political Science
I was learning on his tab.
He suffered my innocence,
knowing, I guess, how a tune
can turn, worm in, begin to gnaw.

The Choir

They sing around a song,
warbly sixty-year-old altos,
nasal tenors, shallow bass
and those screeching sopranos.
What wondrous love is this?
They roil the stream
of Wesley's pen
the way the saved muddy
with baptism a crystal creek.
Their robes, which rolled
from their own shrill
air-jet looms,
glisten, no defects
in the sight of the Lord,
no seconds in this loft,
and this sound is true
as it is off. Twice
now this cloth
has made a joyful noise,
both times for a living.

Looms

Some dragging home from a card game,
some after leaving the hospital where they had sat in the dark beside a bed,
some near dawn, on the way to a cold creek,
some on an early errand to take a dish to a dead aunt's house,
some driving a colicky baby around,
some standing just outside the shaking doors, watching the third-shift moon
    grow pale,
some when an unpaid bill goes again unpaid,
some when an old one going or new one coming calls them out,
some who hope to hang a buck on the old swing set frame before evening,
some squinting and guessing for the center line,
some looking to catch somebody red-handed,
some stalking a son or, worse yet, a daughter
and some not knowing what they seek when everyone else is sleeping

hear them singing,
how they fill up the day ending and beginning for miles.

TWO
Entering the Weave Room

Entering the Weave Room

At the start bell,
they pull the stained handle,
and the great doors
swing open. The blast
is warm, a roaring *hush*.
They step into this lush wind,
like the back draft
from a huge, unearthly flock.

The strings jump in the harnesses
of these clattering, greasy harps,
the music here is
how you make it.

The Men

They'll show you how to milk a mouse.
They'll see if your ears have any gristle in them.
They'd stop in a burning house
to talk about striped bass.
When the lies get serious
they'll take out a knife
and sharpen a stick to nothing.
What they don't say
would fill a book.
You can read it in their shoulders,
in the way their hands find their pockets.
See, they're writing their scripture now,
with one finger,
in the salt that's been spilled
on the tables in the canteen.

The Women

They don't stitch
Bible verses into cloth squares
to decorate sitting-room walls.
They keep their sayings with them,
in the weave room and cloth room,
by the doors of Drawing-In,
at the window to Supply.

They don't have to back up to take their pay.
If you're looking for a fight,
they'll help you find it.
They've got another shift to pull when they get home.
Women work daylight *and* graveyard
all their lives,
and sometimes do it pregnant.

They're the ones, after Revelations,
who fill in the blanks.

Weave Room: What They Say

is mostly lost to the roar of the looms,
the sound they can feel in their soles
as they patrol the alleys
for breakdowns and broken ends.
But they say it anyway,
coming together,
putting a hand on a shoulder,
leaning in,
mouth to ear,
and then mouth to ear in reply,
almost letting lips brush the scalloped cup,
exchanging jokes, flirting, telling secrets,
all in shouts, mostly meaningless,
save for the breath the other can feel,
the warm, damp words like a lotion.

The Informant

It felt cold in his office
because the weave room was warm.

The boy in the gold frame on his desk
smiled in his embrace.

"What are they saying?
Whose talking union?"

The thin cloth of the T-shirt
was like a second chill skin.

"You are my ears," he said,
glancing at the gilted smile.

"I can't hear."
"Then watch and remember."

His arm on the boy's shoulder
was heavy and hot.

Now, a cool stranger in those rooms,
the boy jammed the plugs in his ears,

one of them, not one of them,
he remembered.

Union Summer

For and against,
behind backs, this said,
not that said.

Union talk splintered
softball teams,
congregations,

all that had been together
coming apart
"for the good of all.

How long will you use
up your lives
to make them rich?"

Them. Us.
Behind backs, this said
not that said.

Shop talk ruined
choir practice,
hymns stalled

when bass and tenor
couldn't harmonize
for worldly reason.

"Would you trade
one boss for two?
Pay dues and taxes?"

One for two,
for all,
this said, not that.

Their living rooms
grew raucous with looks.
The wedding wouldn't

take. But the living
with this said,
not that said, the vows

sworn at friends,
not friends, was
for better and worse.

The Singing

Was some thought they could get him to do it
outside the weave room.
They'd call on him in the canteen
or out on the loading dock,
but he said no
that anyone who heard it
would be struck deaf
and wasn't that right, he wanted to know,
since everyone could *see* him
in there anytime with his songs,
but no human ear could hear.
He could be right strange.
Some said he was just mouthing
because no one had ever been able to slip up on him
and catch even a note
and sometimes he would really showboat, making a big *O*
with his mouth and stretching out his right hand
and then clutching his shirt
as though something other than his own hand
had a hold on him.

He would say anything that beautiful,
and here would come that cracked smile of his,
could not even *be* heard
except by dogs, which were really angels
and once, out on the dock,
he proved it to several
when this mongrel came sniffing for sandwich scraps
and he opened up
and no one
heard a thing but
that dog started
whimpering and then rolling around under the dock, howling
until even the jokesters
who said they didn't believe
asked him to stop.
When he did that dog came and licked his hand.
It goes into the cloth he would say.
You can tell by the way it sometimes catches the light.

The Thunderbolts of Zeus

College boy, I learned
how to change a light, 500 times.
My wobbly scaffolding straddled the looms,
and I knelt above weavers and fixers,
pulling out the warm, dusty fluorescent tubes.
Beneath me the warp strings jumped and flinched
like the skin of animals shaking off summer flies.
Beneath me their daily work went on
and only occasionally did they look up
and nod thanks, for my giving light,
letting them see their troubles a little better.
I grew sullen with my Fantastic,
wiping the shades, watched, if at all,
for mistakes, lights left flickering
like distant stars,
annoying them, making them shout up to me
and, of course, I couldn't hear.
This business wasn't exactly occupying
so my mind wandered,
mostly to what I'd read.
I tested the heft of my yard-long light,
my bolt, my glittering message.

They tended their clattering flocks
and should have been grateful,
should have been, I say,
when I gave them new ways to see.

But, of course, they weren't,
carping about how my being over them
just made things more difficult.
So I turned away,
hid my face from them
and thought my lofty thoughts,
"Can a hero have faults?"
bobbled, clutched at and almost caught
the fragile, white tube
before it shattered on one of Mrs. Hambricks' looms,
shearing out the whole warp,
two days work just to get it going again.

And the worst?
Not being on my knees,
picking up my own mess
while their worn soles scuffed
around, everybody coming to look.
No, it was her
hand on my shoulder, her
bending down to me,
smoothing my shirt and
mouthing, "It's alright."
Cursed was easy, forgiven,
almost unbearable.

Meeting

Called a big meeting for a Friday morning. Said we was to meet a man might be interested in buying our plant, man out of New York, or some such place, and when we all gathered, the supervisors and foremen, Mr. Grey introduces him.

He starts with You People this and You People that, saying we ran a tight ship and he admires a tight ship and that's the only way to stay afloat, ha ha, in this industry today. He says he admires our "sense of community," sticking together and not needing a union to speak for us, and then he says he could help us get even more efficient and everybody would profit from that, wouldn't they?

And then Mason Herrick, the one who's always putting a snake in somebody's lunch box or sewing the grease rags together, says why don't we show him the weave room so he can see our operating procedures. Where Mason got words like that is a mystery to me.

So we troop to No. 2 what was running fancy curtains for a New York flipwrist. We start walking the alleys, Mason pointing to different looms like this man knows heddles from drop wires and then Mason leans to him and shouts something. The man looks like he wants to ask somebody else about what Mason said, but he can't figure out how so he shrugs and takes the plugs out of his ears.

Mason pulls us all aside one by one and shows us a note and when we came out of the weave room, it's all agreed. We start mouthing to each other like we're talking big but of course not saying a thing and the man gets ashy colored and we're mouthing "What's wrong?" and he takes off for the office like a turpentined dog heading for home.

Naturally he don't buy the place, but the place, we all say, bought him and then some and what he heard was "a sense of community."

Weave Room: Baptism

The air's kept full of water
to save the yarn.
Every word floats away
like a bubble, soundless.

This drowning is for a living.
At the end of a shift,
they are rinsed in the sound of it,
the smell in their hair
like the musk of the lake.
When they come out,
they find their faithful words waiting.

The Story

"You don't see young ones what talk to they selves so much,"
the supervisor observes.
"Somebody got into her pockets bad."

She told it to her breakdowns, knocked-out ends,
drop wires and whip rollers,
told it to warps and heddles,
her mouth and hands moving together,
working the mistakes, the defects, the ruined pattern.
And she would tell you, if you'd ask or just sit still
in the canteen or the ladies room
or try to scream it to you over the thrash of the looms.
But mostly she told it to herself,
and even she couldn't hear it,
but could feel the words buzzing
like hornets in her chest's angry nest.

Windows

Because they let in
light that would fade the cloth
and, in summer, heat
that would fray the yarn,
they were sealed.
But the newer bricks show
clearly where they had been.

The one I can see through
is in this Friday envelope,
my name cloudy under cellophane.
Behind "Pay to the Order of" I live
and these solid red numbers
show clearly where I've been.

A Weaver

Black warp, purple fill
or bride's white through white,
she watches for seconds.

She watches for broken ends.
She adjusts the whip roller
and jacks the speed.

She will have her break.
She will have her lunch,
her cigarette.

Black warp, purple fill cocktail
or bride's white through white,
she will never have such dresses

or their need.

Union

What I remember of holding my father's hand is that I felt what wasn't as much as what was. Not a single finger had been left whole by his hours at Bald Knob Furniture. And I cannot forget the story the men, his friends, on Needmore Hill told of his first time, at the table saw, only 20, but moving up, no longer tailing the ripsaws, folks already talking of his being made foreman. His left index slipped in, and *prong*, wrong sound of the saw finding something that wasn't wood.

When people looked around, he was sitting, legs spread, in the sawdust his morning had made, clutching a piece of himself so that they had to pry his fingers open to take it from him. And soon after he started talking union.

Never made foreman. When a heart attack found him still at the table saw, the boss said they wouldn't be able to hold his job.

So that's what union talk gets you and when the ACTWU man came sniffing around our softball games like he couldn't see the company name stitched to all our backs, I told him union was just a word and words don't come by with a dish when someone's mother dies and come Sunday he'd find this same gang in the pews at Redwood Methodist and Calvary Baptist and that, my friend, was a blood bond and what a union was good for was getting people fired.

But I began to see the little blue cards around the weave room, men tucking them in shirt pockets, women slipping them into purses. If enough were signed, there'd be no need to vote.

Then the ACTWU started standing outside the gate with leaflets and lettered jackets asking us to choose up teams. More than one who dropped the leaflet when the boss was looking signed the card when he wasn't.

"Did they think Greenville wouldn't notice," I said in the canteen. "New York didn't give a rat's ass whether the cloth came from Angle or Yokohama."

Some said that was right, but others said they wanted more, better, and that I was an ass kisser, looking to make supervisor.

But for or against, we didn't expect what happened. The ties from Greenville coming down the alleys in both weave rooms, shutting off the looms. How many times had we heard it would be cheaper to replace a whole shift than shut off the looms? In both rooms, they were shutting off now, and it was done one at a time, not easy by throwing the main switch, but slow so we would get the full effect.

Then we were invited to the slasher room where they'd cleared out the warp racks and set up tables, covered in good linen. They'd brought in barbecue and tubs of sodas.

Mr. Goldman from Greenville had a few words about our good work, lack of lost-time accidents, and we were told to help ourselves, just help ourselves. And we did, but not to praise or pig but to that sound, that quiet of the looms not running, not what was there, but what wasn't.

The Words

A loom half way up
the 600 alley flashed,
a spark jumping to grease,
and the Hendricks boy,
who had just made fixer,
was under it.
The warp caught fire
and fell on his right arm.
He bucked and rolled
even after the sprinklers
doused the flame.

The old man would say later
he heard the screaming
but that couldn't be,
all those looms running full tilt.
Whatever he heard,
he came slow
like dragging back from break
and moved the supervisor
away from the boy.

There's a half dozen seen this.
He put his mouth close
to the singed arm
and spoke to it all
the way down to the hand.
The boy stopped thrashing,
sat up and after a while
went back to work.
His arm never showed
the first scar.

The old man plodded out
to the broom straw field
on the other side of the parking lot
and bent over like he was sick.
Next morning the field
was scorched black.

Most said a cigarette
thrown from a car
at the end of second shift.
Most said that.

The Preaching

He would pace the 100 alley,
keeping an eye on the sample runs,
checking his looms like The Master watches his flock.
But when he'd really get going
it was hard to think he saw anything,
the way his head tilted back
and his eyes half closed
and he stalked up the alley and back,
working The Gospel over in his mouth,
jabbing at The Truth with his finger.
He didn't even know he was doing it,
his mind was plunged so deep in the idea of God.
It seemed like a fever, his faced flushed,
ears burnished and neck nearly purple
where it met his white T-shirt.
The joke was anybody who wore his cloth
would go off like a Minuteman missile
come The Rapture.
But the supervisor said jokes aside,
he had the lowest defect rate in the whole plant
and they gave him every tricky sample run
and he'd talk it through.

Workers of the World Unite

The scaffold was supposed to roll
but more often than not, threads clogged
the casters and I had to try
to drag it along the loom alleys,
backing gingerly down the ladder
to pull, lift, pull and wait
for one of them to help.
In the canteen, they'd joke,
"Having trouble with your ivy tower, college boy?"
I'd laugh with them, at them,
though they didn't know it.

And once the lanky old guy
who rubbed your shoulder
while he shouted in your ear
called me down
when I was having trouble
feeding the new lights' prongs
into the sockets' slots.
"Put a little hair around that hole
and I bet you could hit it,"
he hooted, hoping, I'm sure
that others heard.

I laughed at all their jokes
because I was above them,
and needed their rough shoves
just to get along.

Lifting

A boyish man, from blond mop
to quick, almost skipping, strides,
he would talk to you
about two things: the mechanics
of lifting and praying.
Mostly he would talk
about both at once.
"It's a matter of slant,"
he'd say, setting the gaff
on a steel-banded cloth box
and yanking to tilt
it onto the dolly
for the run up the ramp
into the waiting truck.
"He's a working little monkey,"
the foreman would say
with some wonder
that a 150-pound man
could levitate 400-pound boxes.
Thick veins bulged in his arms
and pulsed when he readied
to make a pull.

"It's really just paying attention,"
he told me one day
on the loading dock
and just as he said it
a hummingbird jetted up
to a Coke can
someone had left there.
The speck of a bird
paused in the air
as if it were reading
the can's thick letters.
It was holding frantically still.
"There, like that," he said.

How No Lies Were Told

Three months gone,
she started up
in the employee discount store,
at the seconds table,
a kind of singing, keen
like tin ripping in a big wind.
She made for No. 2, screaming,
"No more lies,
I don't want to hear no more lies."
She threw her earplugs in the sand bucket,
went down the 300 alley
and squatted by a sample run.

How they knew,
so quickly and from all over,
they would not be able to say,
but the cloth room emptied,
the canteen, drawing-in.
Women came putting hands to ears,
pushing in the plugs,
volunteering to be deaf.

They came to her
and because they knew
there was nothing
she could hear
they squatted with her,
among those strands
the noise was making
come together.

Mrs. P., Who Worked in the Cloth Room, Became Famous for Her Quilts

Her day's work was inspecting,
the cloth, the men and women,
and her night's work
was undoing all the doings
she witnessed in the day,
those busy mill hands
being the devil's workshop.

She stitched her fiery sermons
against greed, lust,
envy, drinking strong drink
into the seams of quilts.
Tiny letters of thread
sowed brimstone into Lone Star,
Double Wedding Ring
and Trip Around the World.
"O ye generation of vipers,
woe unto you who hear the word
and heed it not."

Some New York collector got word
of her gospel quilts
and seeing them said
he'd pay big money
to preserve her "primitive art."

She wrote her messages,
sometimes all night,
into those warm pages
to cover a thousand sinners
and ruined her eyes
married to that work,
growing rich, living poor,
not even noticing
her threadbare dresses
and the bony body peeking through.

In the Break Room

"What good now?"
she cries at the orange canteen table,
her hands, in spasms, like claws,
even in the braces the doctor said
would help the carpal tunnel.

"They'll let me go,"
she says as though she were a balloon
and her only string,
the thing that kept her where she wanted to be,
was her doing what she knew how to do.

"What good now?"
she whispers to the pale face of the clock,
the sandwiches, nabs, sodas and cakes in their slots,
the salt shaker, the pepper, her own betraying hands.
"What good now?"

Safety Meeting: What Counts

"Horseplay is for horses; it belongs in a pasture. We've operated 1,040 hours without a lost-time accident. At 10,000 hours everyone receives a jacket with their initials stitched in fancy white script. But a lost-time accident will reset the clock. Any questions?"

"You mean if someone gets hurt we start back at zero?"

"With an accident, we start at zero."

"OK. Let's say I'm jerked in a loom, made into panty hose and wind up on Raquel Welch's ass. Does it count that I'm still on the job even though I'm having a good time?"

"As I said earlier, horseplay is for horses."

"How much time for the Coleman cooler?"

"20,000 hours."

"What counts as lost-time?"

"More than one hour off due to a work-related injury."

"Less than an hour isn't lost-time?"

"Not in the eyes of the company."

"So if I work five minutes of every hour, I've worked an hour, in the eyes of the company?"

"It only counts for injury."

"What color are the jackets?"

"How big does it have to be to count as a horse?"

A Fixer Quits

In the fluorescent glare,
every tally mark of grease
on his pants and work shirt shimmers,
as if his clothes were some ledger of worth.
He has left the roar of the weave room,
stalked through Supply
and entered the cool hush
of the front office.
Here he was hired
and hasn't been back since.
Here is his perfect attendance,
his accumulated sick days,
his unused vacation
like a month of Saturdays,
his record of being
of use to the J. P. Stevens Company,
to the Stevens family,
to the clattering, greasy economy
and the production of nylon undergarments
that *snick* like scissors
when the secretary's thighs kiss
as she comes with his files.

Filaments from the looms cling to him,
the cleanliness, the sudden cool,
the sidelong looks
from the bookkeepers grab,
but he notices that on the well-buffed floor
there is a shine
and with the thrash of 400 looms
that shine shakes

and that's all it takes.

Gear Bath

This tin tub
would dissolve a newborn.
Here the knuckle joints
and arthritic elbows
are soaked with Varosol,
eased of their grease.

Rubber gloves almost to the shoulder,
rubber apron,
she swabs their ancient hurts
with a pungent balm.
Almost lovingly, she bathes,
gets them ready to work again.

The Gift

Brooks, the fool, had brought up union and words were coming from the backs of throats the way dogs, before a fight, swallow their growls. So the old man, fooling no one, pipes up with his claim.

"I can find water with a willow branch."

There was back and forth on that and someone says, "Put him to the test," so we cleared the canteen for the parking lot.

He drew the wand from behind his pickup seat. It was a spindly thing, a rickety Y. He held it lightly, level with his belt, and seem to let it lead.

Some chuckled when he started.

Halfway across the lot, the wand dipped like a bird's sharp beak sipping from a puddle.

Some said he did it, and others how would we know if he did or didn't.

He handed the branch to Brooks, the loudest doubter, and walked behind him toward the spot.

Brooks laughed when nothing happened and stood, saying "I told you" to the baying crowd. But the old man reached suddenly and touched Brooks's shoulder. The stick bobbed. The doubter could not believe his own hands and dropped the wand as if it were hot.

We shook our heads and wondered all afternoon but weeks later had nearly forgot until the maintenance crew splashed orange paint to mark the water line before making some repairs. The blazes proved what he had known and had shown to us to cool the angers of our making a living.

A Dress and Some Sheets

In her sixth month,
she found them
in a bag with her name pinned on,
by her pocketbook in the locker room.
The dress, homemade with perfect stitching
only one or two there could have done,
and the sheets, 250 count, first run,
the best they made.
No other card
and no one would say
who or why
though she knew
it was from all of them
because they were hers
and she was theirs,
the best they made.

Notes, Angle Plant, July 1978

Was told today that a woman in the cloth room could remove warts by speaking to them.

They spend their working lives with ears plugged, speaking in their invented languages. Flashlights. Hand signs. Facial expressions.

Working the softball games, very popular, but the company has stamped every shirt with its name, even bat bags. Will attend various services.

Pauline called, Father completely deaf now.

No AC, nights not much cooler than days, through my window I can hear the plant like a distant train.

Must admit the smell of honeysuckle nearly overwhelms me with loneliness. Lonely Union Man. It could be on their awful radio.

Attended Methodist revival. Extremely hot and baffling. The Bible Belt is made of snake skin. Faith of our Fathers alright, the ones that basked on mud banks in the first swamps.

Woman who takes off warts sympathetic, a possibility. God, I need one.

Landlady baked me a pie. Who are these people?

Father stares out window endlessly, Pauline reports. Seems more alert than ever. Happy for first time in years.

Invited to speak, finally!

Coffee with Rev. Albert Muse. Barely understood a word. What is creasy?

Must be offhand, image rich like poetry. Their natural conversation.

Pauline says Father walking to park daily. "A squirrel's eye is a black dime." He has never spoken like that before. Should I worry?

Spoke to Wart Woman about "giants" of the movement. "Well, a tall man's handy when the water's deep." Over my head. She noticed my left hand.

Speech a failure. Foreign language. Mine and theirs. One month and only a handful of cards signed.

Rev. Muse asked about "negroes" in leadership. He said negroes. Apparently, I've lost my muse. Honeysuckle. Honeysuckle. Honeysuckle.

Town deserted after 8 p.m. Late last night teenagers shouted as I jogged. Fortunately, I don't even understand the insults, but the tone was unmistakable.

Father spry. Pauline's word. Talking of touring Civil War battlefields. May have to hospitalize.

Filed complaint with NLRB. Plant personnel officer cited.

Wart Woman chilly. Attends church with personnel officer.

Supplied beer for after softball. Few takers. Man who for all the world looked pregnant said "Ain't the place, boy, beer's for the river bank. After dark."

Personnel officer hit grand slam.

Landlady gives tip. "Folks would listen if you'd get shed of your accent." MY accent!

Found NPR station. Could barely receive but heard some Bach. Praise Jesus, as they say.

Father enjoys watching Dolly Parton. I say it's because he can't hear. Sister needs my help.

Wart Woman spoke to left hand today. A mumble. Primitives.

Company expanded canteen. Gave cash "safety awards." Plant-wide free dinner, all shifts. So Blatant!

Father talking marriage! Ida Mae who has come north to live with her daughter. Will not sanction union. Ida Mae!

Four people tore up cards. "Company treatin real good now." Idiots.

Wart Woman says plant just not ready. Brought me ham biscuits. Says not to feel bad.

I have resigned. This plant will not be organized until a Gideon is raised up from among them. Oh God listen to me. Must be honeysuckle.

Tonight my life is in fourteen boxes. Polishing off softball beer. Home tomorrow. Father happy. Learning to read Ida's lips. Agreed to marriage. And the wart, I swear, is smaller!

All Before Break Time

He's thinking this morning of the taste
of water from a tin dipper,
the metal tang of it,
the memory on his tongue.

He has two breakdowns.
The sample run keeps dropping ends.
He's got too many seconds,
the memory on his tongue.

The warp truck is coming with a new warp.
He's never seen this pattern order before.
The drop wires keep knocking off the loom.
What is this used for, he wants to know.

Water that tastes like where it's been.
What is all this coming together?
What is this used for?

A Union

In the weave room it's always about to rain, the air drenched with mist so the yarn won't ravel. Some of us thought that explained it, reminding him too much of those jungles. The boy was half crazy *before* he went overseas and found the other half.

Some didn't want him hired, the way he'd stare and look over your shoulder when you spoke to him. Needs help we all said though nothing we knew of would help him.

So when he comes strolling down the 400 alley in No. 1, calm as if coming down a church aisle, relaxed with the rifle, looking better than he had, easier in his mind, we were scared but not shocked.

The supervisor, a skittish man in the best of times, takes off for the office and everybody else is ducking behind looms or into the Supply Room if they can make it without crossing his view.

But Mandel Muse, he's a vet too, starts walking slow down the alley, holding his hands down and to his sides, looking him in the eye the way you do with a mean dog to keep him from lunging.

He levels the gun at Mandel's chest. Mandel stops, but holds his gaze. The boy tilts his head to one side and then the other, like a bird stunned when it smacks plate glass.

He's fixing to shoot Mandel, I truly believe, when that girl, that ruined girl, seven months gone, comes down the next alley. She never slows or pauses, never hitches her step like she has nothing to fear or nothing to lose and she marches right up to him, holds out her arms the way you do when you want to take a baby.

He takes her hand and they walk down the alley to the double air doors which swing open and then shut and the roar comes back. I hear it new, like it was the first time, and I notice the lights trembling from the loom shake. It's so loud that not even the crack of the scared deputy's pistol can come in to us. And he fired twice.

Message Lights

When there's a phone call or the plant manager needs to see you, your sequence flashes on the lights that hang all through the weave room. Wouldn't do no good for a bell to ring or people to shout, the room's too loud for that. They're just plain bulbs, 100 watt, on long, dusty cords.

My sequence, only supervisors have them, is three blinks, a pause, then two more, and this afternoon when it came I knew it wasn't a pattern change or unannounced safety meeting. I knew it was a call that I didn't want to receive and so I let it repeat like something I didn't understand, like somebody saying something in a foreign language, a language with words too quick to get.

When Mr. Grey came out to the weave room and put his hand on my shoulder and leaned to my ear and shouted, "We. Need. To. Talk," I just followed him up to the office. The air conditioning made it cold. The deputy was in Mr. Grey's office, the skinny, sneaky-looking one, the one whose pants touch him only at the waist, and I hated him for that, for being so thin like he might break or have to sit down which I did as he was saying he was sorry, and Mr. Grey was saying he was sorry but the boy did have a rifle and with the union trouble and then I thought I could hear everyone back

in the weave room yelling my boy's name, calling him hard and the floor
was shaking and that is all I remember until now, here in the yard, with
the stars winking through the limbs of the dogwoods and I don't understand
what they are trying to say.

Trading Out the Drapers

"Cannibalize" was the word,
whatever parts could be saved
for the plants still using them,
and one or two sent whole
to the plant in South Boston,
but the rest were just scrap.
Some said they'd make anchors
for docks at the lake.
The new air jets, Nissans,
were faster, a little quieter
and had no shuttle.
Some took the old steel-tipped
shuttles for ashtrays, flower
arrangements, but that seemed wrong.

What nobody expected
was that the big air jets
shimmied too much on the floor.
Had to rip out that heart of pine
and pour concrete.
I did take the boards

I'd walked all those years,
those planks varnished
since the plant ran silk
way back before my time.
I made a stool
and when the house is quiet
and my feet are up,
I can see the path
the moon makes on water,
like an unspooled bolt,
shimmering, well-made.

The Living

He went to all their funerals,
"His People,"
made kin by what they did
for a living.

I was his, theirs
for this summer, the next,
this summer the crazy boy
brought the rifle, this funeral
to all,
them, us, me, him,

hands in our pockets,
speaking quietly,
the mother nodding, not looking,
at those bending to offer
a few words,
hands on her shoulder,
mouths to her unhearing ear.

"See what a union does,"
he said to the dashboard.
Did he mean the dying
or the coming together for the living?
"See?" He looked to me
for what? An explanation?
A reply? To name names?
To make sense?

My silence took us home.

The Weaving

The noise of the place,
the roar of its making
sheets, drapes, robes,
lining, outerwear,
even parachutes,

brings them together
men and women not
husband and wife,
women and women,
men and men,

cheek to cheek, almost
kissing, hands to shoulders,
backs, all our possibilities,
as they are not
outside this room's weaving.

The Day Ending and Beginning in the Afternoon

Because they never finish,
they quit at 4, having started
at 7 with 30 minutes for lunch
and 15 minutes for morning and afternoon break.
Second shift will wander in,
gradually a few more in the canteen,
a few in the changing rooms,
a few having a smoke on the loading dock.
Some come half an hour early
to gossip over Cokes and coffee,
to take their ease about punching in,
and one or two run in,
pinning on a hairnet
or making themselves stroll
through the smolder of the supervisor's gaze.
The stragglers meet the swarm
the 4 o'clock bell releases,
grown men and women running for the parking lot,
the gates, the evening to come.
But there are a few
who have washed up and patted a damp paper towel
on their necks and run a finger under watchbands
to ease a day's worth of pinching

and now they sit on a wooden bench,
backs to the wall throbbing with the continuous life
of supply meeting demand.
They watch the parking lot empty
and look out through the chain-link
at the sumac and scrub pine
that border corporate property.
Gum foil glints in the parking lot.
Sparrows notch the fence.
These few are in no rush to get on with it
or get it over.

THREE
Threads

On the Roof of the Angle Plant

Summer was slack,
a dog chain with its dog gone.
I could listen to cricket chirr
and dove moan,
to traffic, such as it was,
on Tanyard and Main
up to The Hub, past Lane Furniture.

This day
I'd been sent to patch the flat roof,
and was idling until my life
could go on with its business.
I'm watching the laze
of ten o'clock Wednesday
make its rounds.
There is Randall Wade's house
on the corner of Pell and Main,
and there is Randall Wade
in the third grade, telling me a circus
with a magic show
was opening in the Lane parking lot
behind his house.

Because I lived in the county
and thought anything could happen in a parking lot
I believed that lie
and believed him that the magician
would spend the night at the house
on the corner of Pell and Main.

It was my first time with such,
a wanting to be liked so strong
that Randall was willing to risk any stretch.
His old dog comes around the house,
untied since age has taken away any desire
to chase cars or bother passersby.
Wednesday sniffs at the corners
and isn't interested.

Mrs. Hudson, the geography teacher,
is in her last year and making a day of the laundry.
She has herded three generations
of landlocked ignorance toward the horizon
and now works to cover the ground
from her backdoor to the clothesline.
The sheets billow for Mozambique or Calcutta,
dragging the morning past the zinnias.
A sudden shift catches her,
wraps her in white, a rustling like wings.
She struggles to keep her footing in the fenced backyard.

I study the pigeon-spiked water tower,
the skyline, such as it is,
the pate of Bald Knob
and lush of Grassy Hill,
the morning taking its time
to break time
and think my life, like an angel,
will descend from that roof.
Then the old dog coughs out a bark,
and the spell is broken.

First Job

Graduated and disguised
by Sear's tie, pen and notepad
as a professional with words,
I covered town meetings,
car wrecks, hail storms,
and the summer's largest zucchini.

Since not working was big news,
I was assigned the story
of the factories' vacation schedules,
and the mill hands yearly week
of crank bait, sunburn,
and oval-track engine roar.

Hell, I could have written it
without talking to a soul,
but I needed quotes so stopped
by the loading dock at shift change.

I shuffled and cleared my throat,
tugged at the knot of the tie,
suddenly speechless in their gaze
the way I had been inside,
college boy, book-lover, future-
white-shirt and desk-jockey.

"What are you planning," I managed
but stopped. My fingers went to the knot
and Brooks smirked. "What's wrong, boy?
You having trouble standing behind that thing?"

The Early Show, Late

Supper cooled.
Mother grew warmer with every lurch
of the minute hand.

Tarzan was teaching
some bad white men a lesson
late in The Early Show,

and I was in no hurry
for green beans and squash,
so I smiled with Cheetah

at everyone getting their comeuppance
or about to.
But it wasn't monkey business

that kept him.
It was the time of day,
work over, long shadows,

a mockingbird covering a lark,
parking lot's asphalt soft
and he'd stopped to talk

about rain or the lack
of it, the color
of the river or its depth

any shallow topic,
better if slightly blue,
near an end like the day.

I know, though I never saw
him do it, tie loosened,
door open to air the car.

I've caught myself now
loitering in a different lot
at the end of the same day.

On the Day the Oldest Textile Mill in the South Closed

Not once did I think of Connor Wray,
that good man, who took me home
after our shift at the Angle Plant,
talking all the way about the day's nothings.
I did not think of the accidental rhyme
of his name with "pay" and "day,"
those working twins,
and so by inattention did one good thing.

I did not think of the fights with my mother,
not fights, she was too calm to call them that,
but her reason made me furious.
My hours at the mill would buy a motorcycle.
"Yes," she said, "they would *or*
see you through a year at school,"
the soothing voice, the placid face
making me rage, "Whose life is it anyway?"

I did not think of Buford Murphy
drawing his knife from its masking tape sheath
to saw the used cardboard cloth boxes
into squares the incinerator could digest.

I did not think of Elton, the jazz fan,
in his hushpuppies and polyester slacks,
accounting for the swing shifts
in the cool of the front office.

I did not think of choir robes,
cocktail dresses, sheets, towels,
draperies, washcloths, suit
lining, upholstery backing,
banners, flags or parachutes,

the forklift, warp truck,
gear bath, reed hooks,
shuttles, spindles, whip
rollers, canteen, vending
machines, punch clock,
parking lot or watertower.

To be honest, I forgot the day
and now try to recall what I did
because I'd meant to mark it.

Probably I worked all morning,
as usual, without speaking,
pushing some words around,
silent as any weaver,
ears plugged, listening,
to my own head's noise.

Any given day, it's like that,
the morning slipping by, the afternoon,
a remembered tune repeating, becoming
annoying, some kid, far off,
shouting, "Whose life is it anyway?"

Threads, End of Another Day

Threads would cling to them,
pants, purses, yokes of dresses,
as they walked or trotted
across the parking lot, released
by the four o'clock bell.

In the building at my back
I could feel the throb of second shift
working the fine strands
that, which was it?, held them up
or held them back from better lives.

Country tunes trailed them out the gate
while I waited for my ride, my evening.
The chainlink trolled those still moments
with its shadow net, and sparrows
gathered the string they let go.

That's it, all that happened, then, there,
and again, here, now, clinging to another day
where I'm working them in.
What you notice becomes your life.